The Inca Civilization

MOMENTS IN HISTORY

SHIRLEY JORDAN

Perfection Learning®

About the Author

Shirley Jordan is a retired elementary school teacher and principal. She is currently a lecturer in the teacher-training program at California State University, Fullerton, California.

Shirley loves to travel—with a preference for sites important to U.S. history. She has had more than 50 travel articles published in recent years. It was through her travels that she became interested in "moments in history," those ironic and little-known stories that make one exclaim, "I didn't know that!" Such stories are woven throughout her books.

Image Credits

T = top, B = bottom, C = center, L = left, R = right

Associated Press p. 16B; Mary Evans Picture Library p. 52B; Robert Harding Picture Library p. 51; North Wind Picture Archives pp. 20, 42, 49; Picture Quest p. 14T; South American Pictures pp. 19, 29T, 38B, 54

ArtToday (www.arttoday.com) pp. 6TL, 6TR, 7B, 8, 10TL, 10BL, 10BC, 10 BR, 11, 12ML, 12B, 13, 14BL, 15T, 16T, 17, 18, 21, 22, 24, 25, 27B, 30, 31BR, 32T, 34B, 35, 36, 38T, 39, 40, 43, 44, 45, 46, 47, 50, 52T, 53, 56, 57, 58, 62C, 62B, 64, 66, 68; Michael Aspengren pp. 23, 32B, 33; Corel pp. 3, 4–5, 6CR, 6BR, 7T, 10TR, 12TR, 15B, 27T, 31TL, 31BL, 34T, 41B, 55, 59, 60, 61, 62T, 63; Shirley Jordan cover, pp. 26, 28, 29B, 41T, 65

Please visit our website at:
www.perfectionlearning.com

When ordering this book, please specify:

Softcover: ISBN 978-0-7891-5405-7 or **3164201**
Reinforced Library Binding: ISBN 978-0-7807-9928-8 or **3164202**
eBook: ISBN 978-1-61384-875-3 or **31642D**

7 8 9 10 11 PP 21 20 19 18 17 16

Printed in the United States of America

Table of Contents

A Timeline of Important Events

5000 B.C.	Bands of hunters/gatherers begin farming on the coast and in the highlands of what is now Peru.
5000 B.C.–1100 A.D.	Various tribes settle the land. They bring their own customs and culture.
1100 A.D.	Cuzco is founded by Manco Capac, the first Inca lord of that capital city. Seven leaders follow him. They enlarge and strengthen the empire.
1438	Pachacuti, the ninth Inca chief, becomes Lord Inca. He enlarges the empire through a series of wars.
1471	Topa Inca begins a vast program of road building to tie the kingdom together.

1498	Huayna Capac extends the empire north into what is now Colombia.
1525	Huayna Capac dies. A civil war follows between his sons, Huáscar and Atahualpa, and their followers. Atahualpa wins and has Huáscar thrown into prison.
1532	Francisco Pizarro invades the Inca lands. He captures Atahualpa.
1533	The Spaniards **execute** Atahualpa.
1535–1537	The Inca empire at Cuzco falls. The Lord Inca, Manco Inca, leads his followers into the mountains. There he sets up his own government. Three of his sons follow him as rulers of the hidden kingdom.
1572	The last Lord Inca, Topa Amaru, is hunted down by the Spanish **viceroy** Toledo. He is executed at Cuzco by Toledo's soldiers. The Inca empire ends.

The Incas Today

*I*f you go to Lima, the capital of Peru, you will find a city much like others all over the world. There are business people, restaurants, movie houses, and crowded streets.

But if you visit the land of the Incas, far up in the mountains, you will find something very different. There farmers still work with simple tools. They grow their crops on terraces hundreds of years old. They gather at the marketplace to exchange fruits and vegetables just as their ancestors did.

In Cuzco, many descendants of the Incas have become tourist guides. They are proud to show visitors their city and the valley where the Incas ruled. If you are lucky enough to go there, they may teach you a few words of the Inca language, Quechua.

Theirs is a fascinating and dramatic history.

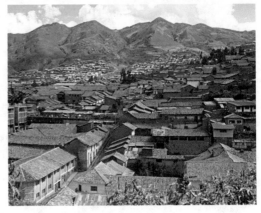

CHAPTER 1

The Incas and Their Ancestors

Over 800 years ago, several tribes of people lived in the Andes Mountains of Peru. The tribes often fought one another. Many times, they raided other tribes' villages.

Some tribal groups lived along the coast of Peru. There the land was like a desert. Other tribes lived in the highlands. Streams were there. But it was very cold at night.

The people in these tribes had many skills. Some groups built cities with walls made of strong stone. Some were known for their beautiful pottery and the cloth they wove. Others found gold and silver on their land. They melted these metals into handsome shapes.

As years went on, a small mountain tribe called the Incas became more and more powerful. They defeated some of the smaller and weaker tribes around them. Before long, they were the most powerful group in the mountain regions.

Each time the Incas defeated another group, they copied their skills. They learned to make stone buildings, pottery, and woven materials. And they discovered how to work with gold and silver.

In the early days, the Indians of Peru were not known as *Incas*. They were given that name by the Spaniards, who heard them speak of their leader, the Lord Inca. It is more likely they called themselves by the name of the language they spoke—*Quechua*.

One hundred years passed. Gradually, the Inca nation became even stronger. Finally, they had conquered all the enemies in their region.

In 1200 A.D., they founded the capital city of their empire. It was in a high valley in the middle of all the land they controlled. So they called it *Cuzco*, a word that means "navel" in the Quechua language. For the Incas, Cuzco was the center of their world, just as the navel is the center of the body.

Now the Incas were so powerful that their forces marched north and south, gobbling up more land. After many victories, they ruled one of the longest empires in the world. Its territory stretched 1,850 miles. It ran from what is now southern Colombia to central Chile.

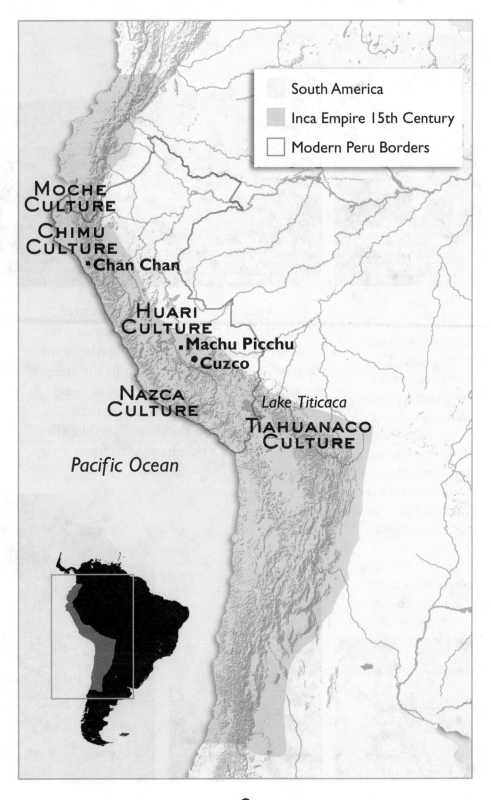

MOCHE
CULTURE

CHIMU
CULTURE
▪Chan Chan

HUARI
CULTURE
▪Machu Picchu
●Cuzco

NAZCA
CULTURE

Lake Titicaca

TIAHUANACO
CULTURE

Pacific Ocean

South America
Inca Empire 15th Century
Modern Peru Borders

The only animals that helped the Incas were llamas and alpacas. They were used mainly for farming. These animals could not carry much weight. But they climbed up and down the steep mountains very well. The Incas also did not know about wheels. So there were no carts. For this reason, their roads did not have to be very wide.

In order to govern such a huge area, the Incas built thousands of miles of roads. To do this, they had to gather tons of paving rocks from high up in the steep mountains. They had no strong animals. Men had to carry huge loads on their backs. Once up on the mountainside, they placed the rocks side by side to form a footpath.

THE PEOPLE OF THE EMPIRE

The Incas ruled their empire from Cuzco. They had conquered many different tribes. And each group of conquered people had its own customs. As long as the conquered people obeyed the Inca laws, they were not forced to change the way they lived. In fact,

Sun Temple at Cuzco

the Incas ordered their prisoners to continue wearing their own clothing. And they were to keep their old hairstyles. This way, a foreign group was easy to recognize.

But there were a few laws for everyone who had been

Ear plug

conquered by the Inca armies. Every man, woman, and child was required to learn the official Inca language, Quechua. They were not allowed to wear gold or silver or large ornaments on their ears. Only the most important Inca leaders could to do that.

Everyone ruled by the Incas had to pay taxes to the government, priests, and local community. The Incas had no system of money. So these taxes were in the form of **tributes** to be delivered to the Inca leaders at Cuzco. Such tributes included cloth, food, crafts, or precious metals.

Every year, each village in the kingdom was forced to send men to work for the government. They built public buildings and roads, fought in the army, or worked in the silver mines. If a man was a farmer, he was forced to work in the fields of the emperor or the priests. And he had to do this after working all day in his own fields.

View of Inca house

But there were benefits to being ruled by the Incas. Old people, widows, and orphans were supported by the government. The leaders in Cuzco made sure everyone had a place to live and enough food to eat. Also, the Incas had storehouses of food saved for times when the crops might fail. And everyone had the protection of the vast Inca army, which grew larger and larger each year.

Inca soldiers

CHAPTER 2

The Religion
of the Incas

Inca men and women prayed to the sun. They called it *Inti*.

The people had several legends about how their tribe began.

One legend said that Inti created a warrior named Manco Capac, along with his three brothers and four sisters. They emerged

from a hole in a hill. The place was called *Paucartambo*. This spot lies about 18 miles from the Inca capital of Cuzco.

Another legend said that Inti created Manco Capac and his sister-wife on an island. Even today, this island is called the Island of the Sun. It is far south of Cuzco, surrounded by the waters of Lake Titicaca.

Manco Capac

13

According to both stories, Inti gave his first Incas a golden **staff** and sent them in search of a special place. He said when they reached the place where they belonged, their golden staff would stick to the earth. Then they would know they had found the chosen place.

Manco Capac

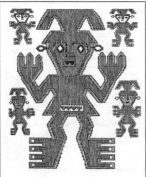

Because the Incas had no written language, their legends were passed from one storyteller to another. When the Spaniards came, they began to write down such things. But they did not always record facts in the same way.

The story says the group continued traveling north. When they reached the Cuzco Valley, Manco threw down the golden staff. Immediately, it sank out of sight. Thus, Cuzco became the center of the Inca civilization.

Inti was worshipped by every Inca. In the highlands, the nights were cold and dark. The people were convinced that their sun god left the mountains each night when the sun set. Because of the cold Andean nights, they believed he swam all night under the earth.

The chief creator-god of the Incas was Viracocha. His assistants were the gods of the sun, moon, earth, and weather. Because the Incas depended so

14

Coricancha (Sun Temple) at Cuzco

much on farming, these gods were honored the most. The Incas built hundreds of temples in their empire.

The most splendid temple was Coricancha. It was a huge monument to the sun, Inti. Its walls were lined with gold, which the Incas found in their streams. It also contained beautiful silver pieces made from ore brought from local mines.

To further honor the sun, the Incas carved huge stones called *intihuatana*. Each was in the form of a **sundial**. Its shadows were used to track the path of the sun. When the sun cast a shadow on a certain point, the Incas knew the days would be long and sunny. Then it was time to plant their crops. There was an intihuatana in every large village.

The high priest at Coricancha was always a close relative of the ruler, the Lord Inca. This priest was the leader for all the other priests in the empire. Other priests were from noble families. Many of them were also related to the Lord Inca. They were

Intihuatana at Machu Picchu

given responsibility for tending sacred objects. They presided at ceremonies, heard confessions, and made sacrifices.

Sometimes the sacrifices of the Incas were crops set aside for burning to honor the gods. For more important ceremonies, an animal, most often a llama, would serve as the sacrifice.

The Inca religious practices were never as bloody as those of the Aztecs, far to the north of them in Mexico. But when times were bad—illnesses, poor crops, or heavy storms—human sacrifices were sometimes made to the gods.

The sacrifices were boys and girls about ten years old. Girls were chosen by the priests. Boys were offered by their parents. The young victims and their families considered this a great honor. Only the brightest and most healthy young people were good enough to be offered to the gods.

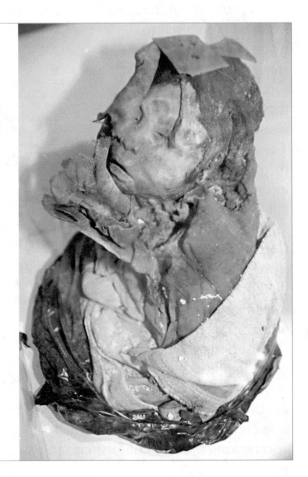

This female mummy was discovered in Inca ruins in the Andes. Twenty-four ceremonial offerings were found with the mummy, including pottery, statues, and food bags.

The girl was about eight years old when she was sacrificed to live with the gods and be worshiped by her people. Archaeologists believe she was unconscious when she died.

The Chief Gods of the Incas

Viracocha	the creator-god. He ruled over all the other gods.
Inti	the Sun and the most important of the sky gods. He created the first men and women on the south shore of Lake Titicaca.
Punchao	solid gold sun-child. Inside the idol was a chalice, or cup, containing dust from the hearts of dead Inca rulers.
Mama Quilla	Mother Moon
Pacha Mama	Earth Mother
Mama Cocha	Mother Water
Cuichi	Rainbow
Ilyapa	lord of Thunder, Lightning, and Rain

HONORING THE DEAD

The Incas believed in life after death. For this reason, they gave great honor to the bodies of those who had died. It was believed that a good person would someday join Inti in the Upper World.

The body of a man or woman who had died was **mummified**. It was wrapped in the finest of clothes. Then it was placed in a sitting position. The knees were tucked up under the chin. Often the feet were crossed.

The Incas did not wrap each arm, leg, finger, and other body parts the way the Egyptians had done. When they wrapped the seated body, they used shawls woven from llama or alpaca wool. A layer

17

of reed mats was often placed over the shawls. In most cases, the head was not wrapped.

For its journey to the afterlife, the body was surrounded by food and personal objects, such as tools or jewelry. In the case of a warrior, his weapons were placed close at hand.

If the body was that of a child, the face was often painted red with yellow stripes. At the young person's feet were three little leather bags. These contained some of the child's hair, clipped fingernails, and baby teeth.

A cave was the usual

Mummy bundle

resting place for an Inca mummy. Family members sealed the entrance to the cave with rocks and mud. Sometimes bodies of other family members shared the burial spot.

THE DEATH OF A LORD INCA

When the Lord Inca died, the whole kingdom mourned. And it was the custom for his wives and all his personal servants to take their own lives. This way they could go with him on his journey to join Inti.

Preparing the body of a Lord Inca was given more care than for an Inca of lesser rank. **Embalmers** removed the inner organs and buried them. The emperor's body was then mummified by the embalmers through various drying processes. Specially trained workers put shells over the eye sockets. These were decorated to look like staring eyes. Jewels and gold were sewn to all his clothing. The emperor's body was left to reside in his house, which now became a holy place.

Meanwhile, the new Lord Inca **fasted** for three days. Then he was crowned, and a great celebration was held. But the new leader did not move into the palace of the man who had died. He had to build himself a new palace in Cuzco.

The mummies of former leaders were given great respect. Each mummy was looked after by servants, just as if it were alive. At special festival times, the bodies were dressed up in the kingdom's most beautiful cloth. Gold and silver ornaments decorated their clothes. Then the mummies of the former emperors were paraded through the streets.

Almost every Inca wore at least one piece of jewelry. This was a pin that held a person's shawl around his or her shoulders. The common people had simple pins of copper or bronze. Important citizens wore shawl pins of gold or silver. These had been carefully crafted by metalsmiths. In death, the shawl pin was used to keep the mummy's wrappings from falling open.

Palace of the princes of Chimu

CHAPTER 3

The Incas and Their Government

*T*he Lord Inca was emperor over all of his people. He was the most powerful person in the kingdom. His people believed he was a **descendant** of Inti, the Sun god.

The Lord Inca's palace was a large group of buildings in the capital, Cuzco. Only important leaders were allowed in that part of the city. There were offices, workshops, and public halls. Large storage areas held all the riches sent as

Ruins at Cuzco

tributes to the Lord Inca.

The buildings where the emperor and his family lived were made of strong, thick stone. They had large rooms and were decorated with paint. Plaques of gold and silver hung on the walls. And the royal family ate from gold and silver trays and bowls.

Without a money system, gold and silver weren't needed to make coins. Instead, these precious metals were always used to create things of beauty.

Incas liked to bathe often. The common people used lakes and streams. But for the Lord Inca and his family, the baths were inside the palace.

The Lord Inca wore clothes made of the best materials. While his government helpers wore clothes made from the wool of llamas and alpacas, the emperor's clothes were woven from the wool of a rare sheeplike animal called the *vicuña*. And he wore his clothes only one time. Then they were burned.

With his fancy clothes, the Lord Inca wore a special braid of many colors. It was wrapped around his head several times. From it hung a royal fringe made of red tassels and shiny gold tubes.

The emperor's main wife was called the *Coya*. The people worshipped her as a relative of the female god Mother Moon. When the Lord Inca was away from Cuzco, the Coya sometimes took his place as ruler.

A Coya

21

Because the royal family wanted to be sure their leader's blood was pure, a Lord Inca often married his sister. Even though he might have other wives, the Coya was honored because one of her sons would become the next Lord Inca.

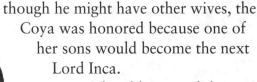

The oldest son did not automatically become the next ruler. The Lord Inca chose whichever son he thought would do the best job of leading the empire. His other sons were trained to govern other parts of the kingdom.

Inca lord

A Vast Empire

As the Inca empire grew in size, it took over the land of almost 100 tribes. The population grew to nine million.

Many more men were needed to govern the tribes farther from Cuzco. Sometimes not enough male relatives of the emperor could be found.

When this happened, young men called *curacas* were chosen and trained to lead. Although not related to the Lord Inca, they were from trusted noble families. The curacas did not have to pay taxes. And to show their importance, they were allowed to wear bright feathered **tunics**. In their pierced ears, they proudly wore large golden spools.

The Incas had a special way of dealing with tribes that had been newly conquered. It was called the *mitima*. In this plan, hundreds of families within the conquered area were forced to move to **provinces** that had been under Inca rule for a long time.

In their place, a group of Inca families, loyal to Lord Inca, were moved to the new area to replace them. These transferred citizens taught the new tribe about the Inca culture and religion. And they trained the new citizens in Quechua. **Artisans** and farmers taught crafts and methods of agriculture.

To reward the loyal citizens moved in the mitima program, the Lord Inca ordered special favors for them. The government gave them gifts of gold and silver, feathers, and cloth made of llama and alpaca wool. The men were allowed more than one wife.

The Incas did not have a written language. But they did have a well-developed communication system. To keep all parts of the kingdom informed, the government depended upon thousands of *chasquis*—Inca post runners. These swift messengers relayed throughout the road system that wove out from Cuzco.

LET'S MEET PACAL,
ONE OF THE YOUNG POST RUNNERS.

Two years ago, Pacal was chosen to be a chasqui. He is proud of his important work. He remembers when he was younger and how hard he practiced on the road near his village. None of the other boys could keep up with him. Everyone said Pacal ran like the wind.

Just like other chasqui runners, Pacal has a special part of the Inca road that is his responsibility. It is about two miles long. Every chasqui can run that far at top speed.

Pacal's bare feet know every stone along the way on his part of the road. He can run it day or night, even when there are no stars.

It is morning, and Pacal has just gotten up. He steps outside his cone-shaped hut and stretches his arms and legs.

Pacal is always sad when he says good-bye to his family as he leaves for this hut by the road. But chasqui runners are on duty for 15 days at a time. They must live close to the trail so no time will be lost.

As Pacal turns to go back into his hut, he hears a sound. It is the haunting tone of a **conch** shell. A runner is coming with a message. Pacal must be ready to start out on his run.

Quickly he gathers his sling and some rocks of the right size. In his other hand, he will carry a hand weapon called a **mace**. Chasquis are not attacked by strangers very often. But it is important to be ready.

The runner with the conch shell runs up to the doorway. "I have some news of another tribe near the coast," he says. "The Lord Inca wants to know whenever strangers are near."

"I will hurry with the message," says Pacal. He takes the conch shell from the other boy. It fits into a pouch on his back. He also reaches for a small, wet bundle wrapped in a cloth of reeds.

So swift were the chasqui runners that they have been thought to run their two miles in about 13 minutes over rocky paths.

Each morning, there is such a bundle to carry. The Lord Inca eats fresh fish from the sea once each day. The fish are caught 150 miles from Cuzco. So the chasquis must run their relays very swiftly. It would not do to bring spoiled fish to the Lord Inca!

Soon Pacal is racing along his part of the trail. Before long, he will blow the conch shell to signal his arrival at the next hut. He will tell the relay runner about the strangers on the coast. And he will hand over the Lord Inca's dinner fish.

Pacal makes his breath come slowly in the high mountain air. He steps in just the right places to keep from tripping. As he runs, he smiles to think of how important his job is to the Inca nation.

24

The Lords of Cuzco 1200–1437

Manco Capac legendary son of Inti. He founded the capital at Cuzco.

Sinchi Roca son of Manco Capac. He designed the forehead fringe of red tassels worn by all Lord Incas.

Lloque Yapanqui son of Sinchi Roca. He resisted attacks by other tribes in Cuzco's valley.

Mayta Capac son of Lloque Yapanqui. This strong warrior was said to be influenced by **wizardry**.

Capac Yupanqui son of Mayta Capac. He was the first Lord Inca to send warriors beyond the outskirts of Cuzco to demand tribute.

Inca Roca son of Capac Yupanqui. He founded a four-year school for boys of high birth and began the practice of training "Chosen Women."

Yahuar Huacac son of Inca Roca. He was kidnapped as a child, but released. He married princesses from neighboring tribes.

Viracocha son of Yahuar Huacac. He began the conquest of all the Cuzco Valley. He named himself after the creator-god of the Incas.

Rulers of the Inca Empire Before the Spanish Conquest 1438–1533

Pachacuti son of Viracocha. He was a mighty conqueror. He added to the kingdom by a series of conquests, 1438–1471.

Topa Inca son of Pachacuti. He continued Inca conquests, 1471–1493.

Huayna Capac son of Topa Inca. He **expanded** the empire northward. He died of the plague in 1527.

Huáscar son of Huayna Capac. He was overthrown in a civil war in 1525 and then ordered executed by his brother, Atahualpa, in 1532.

Atahualpa son of Huayna Capac. He was captured and executed by Francisco Pizarro in 1533.

CHAPTER 4

The Incas As Farmers

◻◻◻◻◻◻◻◻◻◻◻◻◻◻◻

*F*armland was of many different types. Most land was mountainous. The Incas cultivated their crops on farms as we do. But their farms and crops had to be right for the different kinds of land. Different crops were needed for different heights above sea level.

Along the coast of the Pacific Ocean, the land was flat. Almost no rain fell. Here the Incas lived in huts with mud-brick walls and flat roofs of straw and reeds. They planted hardy crops like corn and beans.

Since there was so little rain, the farmers needed water from mountain streams. Where a stream flowed down from higher land, men labored to build **irrigation** ditches. These ditches carried stream water to crops on the driest land. Where this was done, the crops grew tall.

Inca water system

Higher up, the land stretched across vast plateaus. These areas were surrounded by three mountain ranges. As clouds floated over the mountains, they dropped rain upon the plateaus.

But the Inca farmers did not want the rain to run down steep hillsides and be lost. And they did not want their fine topsoil washed away. To stop this loss of precious water and land, they built **terraces**.

The job was backbreaking and took many years. Workers fitted together millions of rocks and made walls that would hold back the soil. Then they laid a layer of more rocks behind each wall. After that, they filled in each terrace with soil. This created a flat surface for planting. Like the farmers on the dry coastal land, they directed natural streams from terrace to terrace. Small canals lined with stones brought water to the thirsty plants on the lower terraces.

In some places, the terraces were 15 feet high. To climb to the next terrace, a farmer walked up a series of flat rocks. They stuck out from the side of a wall like stairs.

Terrace steps

What foods did these ancient people grow? Chief among the plants valued by the Incas were *sara* (corn), *chuño* (potato), and *quinua* (a hard-shelled grain product ground into cereal). All three of these farm products could be stored for many years.

Squash, sweet potatoes, peanuts, and beans rounded out the year's harvest on the steep terraces. Closer to their houses, the Incas grew pineapple, papaya, and avocados. Tomatoes, lima beans, and chili peppers sprouted wild in the hills.

Inca farmers worked together for the good of the community. No one was paid because there was no money system. But each worker knew the government would see that he and his family had a place to live and enough to eat.

Farming chores were hard. The Incas had no iron tools. And they did not know anything about the wheel. So there were no wagons. They did not even have work animals to pull a plow. So, carrying pointed digging sticks, a small group of neighbors moved from one man's farm to another. While one farmer dug a hole

Quinua is a hardy cereal plant. It is brightly colored with all the shades of autumn leaves. This plant grows well in elevations from 10,000 feet to the snow line. It survives even with a lack of water. And it can recover from a winter frost.

Even today, bright fields of quinua decorate the Peruvian hillsides. Ground to a powder, this nutritious grain adds flavor to soups and stews.

28

with his stick, other men dropped in the precious seeds and covered them with soil.

The hardworking Incas were careful not to be caught by times of hunger. So greatly did they fear famine or drought that they grew far more crops than they needed.

Inca law said that farmland crops must be used for three purposes. One portion was set aside to feed the farmers and their families. Another portion was used for religious practices. The Inca priests burned these crops as offerings. The final share went to the government.

These government crops were stored in warehouses, waiting for a time of war or famine. To keep their stored food safe, the Incas built their storehouses high into the mountainsides.

Mountain storehouses

Preparing Chuño for Winter

The Incas were the first people on earth to grow and eat white potatoes. In good weather, they dug up the potatoes that were ready and ate them in soups and stews.

When the winter months (June, July, and August) approached, they prepared these potatoes for storage. The method they used kept the potatoes from becoming rotten when they were stored.

The Andes mountains, where the Incas lived, is south of the equator. So they have winter when we have summer. And they have their summer growing season when we have winter.

LET'S MEET KIMA,
A 14-YEAR-OLD BOY OF THE HIGHLANDS.

The morning is cold when Kima awakens. Soon winter will be upon the Andes Mountains where he lives. The deep shadows cast by the mountains block the sunshine around the family's home until almost midday.

The hut where Kima lives with his mother, father, and sister is made of large fitted stones. The walls work well to keep the family warm.

Kima's father and grandfather had been careful workers. Using stone tools, they had built the house many years ago. They had cut each stone just right. Then the large slabs of stone had been placed side by side.

The stones fit so tightly that the wind still cannot blow through the walls. Just one small window lets in light.

The roof is made of thatched reeds and grasses. It slopes down toward the ground. If a winter storm comes, snow will slide off such a roof.

The one door is shaped like a **trapezoid**. The narrow part of the trapezoid is at the top.

Kima rises from his sleeping mat. As in all Inca homes, there is no other furniture.

Kima can hear his father moving about. His mother is building a fire to warm beans for breakfast. She wears a long, sleeveless dress. It is made of material she wove on her **loom**.

In the shadows of the house's one room, Kima's sister, Homma, still sleeps. Near her shoulder, two guinea pigs scamper on the dirt floor. They will make a tasty feast when the family celebrates the harvest. Guinea pigs are Kima's favorite food. And they are the only meat the Incas eat.

Now Kima and his father dress for the day. They wear **loincloths** and sleeveless tunics. When it is time to go outside, each member of the family will put on a woven cloak held

closed by a metal shawl pin. Because they are not nobles, they own no other jewelry.

Kima knows his mother and sister worked many hours the day before. It was their job to cut all the small white potatoes into slices with their stone knives. It is a task that must be done every year in June.

Last night, after the potatoes were cut, the whole family worked together. They spread the potato slices upon the ground, each in its own spot. The job had to be finished before the sun went down.

"Was it cold enough last night?" Kima whispers as he speaks to his father. "Have the potato slices frozen?"

"Yes," his father answers. "I went outside to see. They are well frozen. We can start making them into chuño when the sun is warmer."

Kima sits down by the fire. His mother hands him a clay bowl with some cooked beans. He reaches for a gourd filled with water. Kima's father pours himself some *chicha* for his own breakfast drink.

Homma is up now. She pulls a woven garment of llama wool over her head. It is one she helped her mother make. Homma is learning to weave cloth for the family.

The women go outside. There is much work to do. The sun is coming up over the mountains. Its rays fall upon the frozen slices of potatoes. "It is time," says Homma's mother. The two women begin to gather the potato slices into piles in the morning sunshine.

Kima and his father come out of the house. Now everyone will work. Kima's father places his bare foot upon a pile of potato slices. He raises his foot. Then he stomps down.

The Incas were fond of an alcoholic beverage called *chicha*. It was prepared by the woman of the house. She boiled corn, then chewed the cooked vegetable. As she chewed, the corn mixed with her saliva. This turned the corn's starch into sugar.

The woman put the chewed mass into a large pot, mixed it with water, and boiled it for a short time. Then she set the pot aside for at least a day. As the sticky mixture sat, the sugar slowly turned into alcohol. The result was a cloudy-colored beer.

33

The potatoes have frozen in just the right way. When the night temperature dropped below freezing, the potato slices froze all the way through. This freezing broke down the inner cells of the potato, making the cells easier to burst.

As Kima's father smashes the potatoes with his foot, cold water squishes out of each slice. Soon the women take over the work, pressing bare feet on top of the slices and watching the liquid squirt out. Stomp, stomp, stomp. Over and over they squeeze the slices.

There are many slices, and the work takes most of the day.

Finally, Kima's father gives an extra stomp to each piece of potato. Now he is sure the slices are flat enough.

"Is it time?" Kima's mother asks his father.

"Yes," he replies. "You and Homma can spread these out to dry in the sun now. Then they'll be ready to store. Tomorrow you will slice more potatoes to spread during the night."

Kima is glad the day's work is over. But he knows it will take four more days to have enough chuño to last the winter.

CHAPTER 6

Education and Training

□■□■□■□■□■□■□■□■□

The Incas had no written language. For this reason, going to school was very different for them. It was not like the reading and writing taught to the young people of America or Europe.

And the Incas did not have coins that represented money. Without money, very few people had a reason to learn to count. There was no need to buy anything in Inca times. All things—crops, textiles, tools, and animals—belonged to the Lord Inca and his government.

What the government had was divided among the workers. People who were too old or ill to work were given what they needed. Under this system, there was no middle class, such as merchants.

But even without a written language, the Incas wanted to pass on what they knew. They did this by means of stories, songs, and poems. Repeated over and over, these forms of communication kept knowledge of Inca history and religion alive.

Inca design

All Incas were married by the age of 20. And the people of their tribe hoped they would have large, hardworking families. If young people were too slow in choosing a partner, an Inca official would simply pair them up.

Weaving

CHILDREN OF THE PEASANTS

Sons and daughters of Inca peasants were taught by their parents. Sons learned to join their fathers in farming. Daughters learned to prepare two meals a day, spin wool from the family's llama or alpaca, and weave blankets and clothing for the family.

During some weeks of the year, the women might help with harvesting crops. In June, mothers and daughters would be busy making chuño from the harvest of white potatoes.

Young men were assigned other tasks that served the government. Each one paid his tax by working in the mines, building bridges and temples, or serving in the army. Serving in the army of the Lord Inca was a favored job. Going down into the dirty and dangerous mines was a job few wanted.

Warriors

DAUGHTERS OF THE NOBILITY

In Cuzco, the capital city, some of the girls were chosen as "Brides of the Sun." Another name for them was "the Chosen Women." Usually these girls were eight years old or younger. Each was known for her beauty and her good family.

The "Chosen Women" lived in **convents**. They were taught by *mamacunas*, older women similar to nuns. The young girls were taught spinning, weaving, sewing royal garments, and making holy bread.

Some spent their whole lives in the convent. They took vows of service to the sun god and never married. Others became wives of the Lord Inca or his noble assistants. A few stayed in the convent to become mamacunas to younger girls.

Less beautiful young girls and those from poorer families did not go to the convent. They were trained at home by their mothers. They learned to cook, weave, and care for children. All of them were married before they were 20 years old.

SONS OF THE NOBILITY

Each year, Inca officials chose a number of boys from good families. They had the chance to attend a four-year school that had been founded long ago by the Inca Roca. They studied for four years, orally learning their nation's history, religion, and language.

Before the years of training began, a young man went through 30 days of events to mark his entry into manhood. This period might include a llama sacrifice and sporting events, such as foot races. Each young man received a hunting sling made of braided llama wool. With it, he could hurl stones at an animal or bird with good success. The slings, when used with a metal shield, would later become important in his training as a warrior.

For the final ceremony of his coming to manhood, a priest gave the young man a new name to use as an adult. Then he pierced the boy's earlobes with a large thorn. Over time, these ear holes would stretch larger and larger so that someday they would hold huge ear disks of gold or silver. Sometimes these decorations were as big as a compact disk.

When the conquerors came from Europe, they called the nobles with stretched ears *orejones*. In Spanish this means "big ears."

In the school, boys learned a method the Incas used to remember important numbers. Without a written language, there were no account books. Instead, certain educated Incas used a system of numbers involving knotted and colored strings called *quipus*. These might be used to count the population. Or a quipu might be the record of how much food was stored for winter.

For important records, the strings on a quipu might be ten feet long. And it might have as many as 2,000 strings. A young man who wanted to spend his life keeping quipu records for the government could become a *camayoc*. This would be like the job an accountant does today.

CÕTADOR·MAIOR·ITEZORERO
TAVANTINSVIOQVIPOC
CVRACA·CON DOR·CHAVA

The Craftsmen

Some young Incas had special talents in arts and crafts. If chosen for their skill, they worked full-time for the Lord Inca.

A young man might be especially good with stone or metalworking. He would be one of a few chosen each year to work for the government as a craftsman. He learned to melt the gold and silver found in the streams and mines.

The young man built a very hot fire in a clay furnace. The metal was placed in the furnace. When it was hot enough, the metal turned to liquid. Then the liquid was poured into clay molds. Dishes, vases, statues, and jewelry were made this way.

The Incas discovered how to melt copper and tin together to make bronze. This gave them a stronger metal to use for tools and weapons.

Such a craftsman was not a slave, however. Some of them were later promoted to important government jobs.

THE WEAVERS

Most of the Incas who made textiles were women. And weaving for each family's clothes was done at home.

A young woman might be especially good at designing and weaving fine fabrics. Then she could become a worker for the Lord Inca.

First, the weavers spun threads—cotton ones from cotton plants and wool threads from the wool of llamas or alpacas. When the threads were ready, the women dyed them bright colors, such as blue, red, and yellow. Then, on small hand looms, they wove the colored threads into tunics, **ponchos**, and blankets. If the cloth was for an important official, brightly colored feathers might be woven among the threads. Designs on the cloth were often geometric shapes—triangles, diamonds, and squares.

The Incas made their most beautiful and valuable cloth from the wool of the *vicuña*. The craftsmen chosen for this task were specially trained male weavers or the mamacunas who guarded the Chosen Women. If the garment was for the Lord Inca, it would be worn only once. Then it was burned.

THE STONE MASONS

The Incas were gifted engineers and stone workers. They built government buildings and homes for the citizens. Their work is most notable for how solid it was. Using stone tools and bronze levers, workmen made buildings with walls of huge granite blocks. They used no **mortar** to **cement** the pieces.

If a rock was too large or did not have the right shape, the Incas had to cut it. First, they scratched a line where they wanted to cut the rock. Then they scratched more and more to widen the mark. Next they chipped some holes along the line.

Each cold night, they dribbled water into the crack. Then the crack and holes were filled with wet grass. As the water on the wet grass froze, it expanded. This forced the rock apart at the line. It took many nights before the rock would split in two.

Somehow these early people fitted their giant blocks together so closely that, even today, a knife cannot be inserted between the stones. The walls have even resisted centuries of earthquake activity without falling down.

Just outside the capital city of Cuzco is a huge fortress called Sacsahuaman. Its three long rows of walls were built to protect the city from attack. It was ordered by the Lord Inca Pachacuti in the 1450s.

Sacsahuaman

It is difficult to imagine how men, with few tools, could have formed such a fortress. The rocks had to be gathered from a **quarry**, hauled to the city, and set in place. Some of these rocks weigh as much as 100 tons! Historians believe it took 30 years and 20,000 men to complete Sacsahuaman.

THE BRIDGE BUILDERS

As the Inca empire grew, it became important to get from place to place. Many times the easiest way was to cross a river. The rivers of the Andes are filled with dangerous rapids. Many people drowned trying to cross. But to go around the rapids meant journeying an extra hundred miles.

To span the rivers of the empire, the Lord Inca Pachacuti ordered **suspension bridges** to cross the rivers. These bridges had to be tightly attached to the mountainsides. So the Incas built huge stone columns on both sides of the river. Sometimes craftsmen braided plant fibers of *coyo*, a tubular grass, into ropes. Other times they used the fibers of the *maguey* plant. Both were very strong. When the braided ropes were ready, they were twisted into cables as thick as a man's leg. The ends

were attached to the stone columns on each side of the river.

Once the span was in place, workers built rope sides to form a cagelike wall on each side. Other ropes acted as a railing for those walking across.

These bridges lasted about a year. It was the job of the citizens of nearby towns to make repairs or build new suspension bridges when needed.

Spanish Conquerors Come to Peru

In 1522, Francisco Pizarro was mayor of the city of Panama. He was already more than 50 years old. His career in Spain's army had been an exciting one. He had served bravely.

Among Pizarro's memories was his service under Hernán Cortés. They had fought together to conquer the lands of the Aztecs in Mexico's Valley of the Sun. And Pizarro had struggled across the mountains with Vasco Nuñez de Balboa. They had been the first to gaze upon the Pacific Ocean.

Pizarro was born in Trujillo, Spain. Historians believe the year was 1471. But his parents were not married. So no one had bothered to register the birth. When he was a few days old, his mother abandoned him.

Francisco Pizarro

His grandparents raised Francisco and his four half-brothers—Juan, Hernando, Gonzalo, and Martín.

With no schooling, Francisco could neither read nor write. It seemed impossible that he would grow up to be a leader.

But Francisco Pizarro worked hard. He rose in rank in the Spanish army. Later he signed on to a ship bound for the New World. Once there, he never again dreamed of living in Spain.

Now he was older than most soldiers of his king. Pizarro longed for adventure.

Rumors were spreading through Panama. A land to the south held much gold, the stories said. Pizarro could be still no longer. It seemed the riches were waiting just for him.

In 1524 and again in 1526, Pizarro sailed south in search of gold and silver. He reached Colombia on the first expedition and Ecuador on the second. But he did not have enough men and supplies. He was forced to turn back both times.

In November 1532, Francisco Pizarro was back. He led

an army into the mountains of northern Peru. With him were 62 men on horseback, 105 foot soldiers, and one Catholic priest. His four half-brothers were among his officers.

King Charles I of Spain had just appointed Pizarro governor and captain general of Peru. He was to explore the mountainous land. And he was to lead the Incas into the Catholic faith.

Pizarro must have been a convincing man. When King Charles named him governor of Peru, the king did not own it. It is likely that the

Pizarro and Charles I

king also did not know that these new lands were twice the size of Spain.

Pizarro had been planning his march for almost ten years. He had many fine titles. But he had little money and military strength.

He was eager to succeed. Like earlier Spanish invaders, he was driven by a greed for gold. But he also had faith in the holy wars now being waged by Spain. He and his men called themselves *Christians*. They would convert the Incas to their religion.

Pizarro's flag was decorated with the picture of a llama. This must have seemed like a proper symbol to the Spaniard and his followers because the Andes was home to the wooly, long-necked animal.

Pizarro's 168 Spaniards were marching into the lands of the Inca leader, Atahualpa. This great-grandson of Pachacuti had finished a bloody civil war against his brother, Huáscar. The civil war had taken the lives of thousands of Incas on the battlefields of Peru. Now Huáscar was in prison, and Atahualpa had won the throne.

Atahualpa

The new Lord Inca had huge armies. Some historians have said he had between 30,000 and 80,000 men. How could such an army possibly lose a war against a few Spaniards?

Were Pizarro's men prepared for battle? It is hard to imagine how they could have been. Each man carried only his own sword, his shield, and a small bag of food. The troops had only a few primitive firearms.

Their march took more than a week. The Andes Mountains of Peru were very steep. The horsemen often had to dismount and lead their steeds.

Pizarro began to enjoy an advantage on this march. Many Incas along the way were unfriendly with Atahualpa. They joined Pizarro's forces.

When Pizarro and his followers were still 1,000 miles from the sacred valley of the Incas, they learned something from their scouts. Atahualpa and his armies were away from Cuzco. Instead, they were camped in a broad, high valley called Cajamarca. This was much closer to Pizarro's position. Many miles would be cut from his march.

At Cajamarca, natural wells bubbled with hot water from far below the ground. Steam rose across the valley from these hot springs. Atahualpa and his men had gone there to enjoy the baths. They were camped nearby in row upon row of brightly colored tents.

Using ancient Inca trails, Pizarro and his men reached the mountain above the valley. They stopped in fear and amazement. Seeing thousands of tents, the Spaniards judged that at least 50,000 Incas were camped in the valley below.

But Pizarro would not turn back. He was almost 60 years old. He had lived twice as long as most warriors. And he was impatient.

Spaniards believed combat was the only way to gain honor. Yes, they were badly outnumbered. Pizarro could only hope that the advantage of having men on horseback would even the odds.

If the sight of thousands of Incas alarmed Pizarro, he could not let this be known. With him were men from native tribes, who were unfriendly to Atahualpa. If angered or disappointed in Pizarro's leadership, there were enough of them to take control of his army. They themselves might rise up and kill the Spaniards.

Pushing forward, Pizarro led his men down into the valley of Cajamarca. They struggled to keep their footing in the narrow passes. The high altitude made them short of breath.

Pizarro, his soldiers, and his native allies finally reached the town at Cajamarca. They found the Inca tents empty. Atahualpa had taken his army to the hot springs, four miles away.

A Clash Between
Two Proud Leaders

It was not long before Atahualpa's messengers brought him news of the Spaniards. Quickly, the Inca ruler sent a messenger, bearing gifts to Pizarro. In reply, Pizarro sent two military leaders, each with 20 men, to the Inca camp. After an uneasy conversation, the king agreed to accept their invitation to visit Pizarro the next day.

For Pizarro, the next day passed slowly. He paced along the mountain path. He needed a plan. Meanwhile, Atahualpa was preparing to show his might by parading across the plain to meet the Spaniards.

Pizarro was desperate for a strategy. At last, he decided upon a bold trick. His few soldiers could not possibly defeat the thousands of Incas. Instead, he would have to capture the king!

His men were terrified at the idea. But they followed orders. Pizarro ordered them to hide in Cajamarca's public buildings—those with doorways high enough for a horse and rider to pass through. This way, they hoped to encircle the Inca king and take him prisoner.

Early the next afternoon, Atahualpa started across the plain toward the town square. He was dressed in his finest robes and seated in his golden litter. It was carried by slaves.

Parading with Atahualpa were 3,000 warriors dressed in red. The visit was to be a friendly one. So the warriors were only lightly armed. They chanted and swept the ground in front of their king with palm branches.

Next came hundreds of singers and dancers, shouting triumphantly. Beside Atahualpa's litter, bedecked in parrot feathers, came his chiefs and nobles. Almost 5,000 Inca nobles, soldiers, and performers were soon crowded into the plaza.

This was the agreed-upon meeting place. But Atahualpa could see no Spaniards. "Where are they?" he demanded.

48

His answer came from one man. The Spanish priest who had traveled with Pizarro's army came forward. He held out his cross and his prayer book. In a loud voice, he began to scold the Incas for worshiping the gods of sun, moon, and water. Instead, they must bow to the Catholic faith.

Atahualpa was furious. He pointed to the sun, then sinking behind the hills. "My god," he said, "still lives in the heavens and looks down on his children."

Spanish priest scolds Atahualpa.

Just then, a blast of bugles filled the air. Guns thundered. As if by magic, the plaza was full of Spaniards in armor. They rushed out from every gate and window.

The terrified Incas were caught by surprise. Pizarro, dressed in quilted cotton armor, ran forward. He swung his sword and advanced toward Atahualpa. With his slashing weapon, he cut off the hands of the king's litter bearers.

Loyal to their leader, the slaves bravely shifted the weight of the litter to their shoulders. At last, they could do no more. The litter crashed to the ground. Spanish soldiers grabbed Atahualpa and hurried him into a nearby building. This was the prisoner they wanted.

As darkness fell, the battle continued. The Spanish horsemen chased down fleeing Incas and ran them through with their swords. Finally, Pizarro ordered his bugler to signal an end to the battle. The Spaniards turned from their fighting and returned to their leader.

It is hard to believe, but not one Spanish soldier had been killed in the daring raid. And the only wound reported was a cut to Pizarro's hand.

Historical accounts list the Inca dead at more than 2,000 men.

A few hours later, Pizarro had regained his courteous Spanish ways. He made sure his prisoner received a fine meal. And to the surprise of the Inca king, Pizarro even sat down and ate dinner with his captive.

A RESTLESS PEACE

From then on, Atahualpa ruled his empire from prison. His many wives were allowed to bring him fine foods. He dressed immaculately, wearing the outfits of his rank. The chiefs from his provinces still considered him their ruler, even though he was locked up at Cajamarca.

But Atahualpa was worried. He feared that his defeated brother Huáscar might somehow escape from prison and strike a deal with Pizarro. So he gave secret orders to have Huáscar killed.

Hoping for freedom to govern his people, the king offered Pizarro a ransom. He indicated a room 17 x 22 feet. This he agreed to fill with gold as high as a man could reach. After the gold

Huáscar

had been removed, Atahualpa promised to fill the room two more times—with silver. He would do all of this within two months.

The Inca peasants were astonished. What could the Spanish possibly want with all that gold and silver? Some even wondered if they ate it.

Slowly, gold and silver for the ransom were assembled. Much of it was obtained by prying 700 plates of gold from the walls of Coricancha, the Temple of the Sun in Cuzco. Other treasures came from the tombs of royal Inca mummies.

In five months, the Spaniards forced the Incas to remove 285 loads of treasure from Cuzco. Some of it was carried by llama to Cajamarca. There were idols, chalices, altars, and fountains. The largest pieces were carried on the backs of men.

The Spaniards cared nothing for the craftsmanship. All the fine metalwork was melted in nine giant fires. The liquid gold and silver were shaped into **ingots** to be carried back to Spain.

Each Spanish foot soldier's share was 45 pounds of gold and 90 pounds of silver. The officers received even more. Pizarro himself took 13 shares of the treasure, plus Atahualpa's 200-pound golden litter.

When the ransom had been paid, the king waited for his freedom. But he was deeply troubled. A comet that was considered a bad sign had passed over the valley. Atahualpa was afraid his luck was running out.

He was right.

He was tried by the Spaniards and sentenced to die. To avoid the usual method of death, burning at the stake, the Lord Inca agreed to be baptized. During the ceremony that followed, he took the Christian name, Juan de Atahualpa, after John the Baptist.

Then, in the great plaza of Cajamarca, the Spaniards garroted the Inca king. That is, they strangled him with an iron collar by slowly tightening its screw.

Atahualpa being put to death

When word of Atahualpa's death reached King Charles I in Spain, he was furious. This was far beyond the power he had granted Pizarro.

Pizarro at the Inca court

Back in Peru, the Spaniards were victorious. But they still did not have the support of the Inca nation. At any time, the Inca natives might rise up to kill the foreigners.

Pizarro needed an Inca to run the country. It must be someone the natives would obey. And that man would have to take orders from Pizarro, the governor of Peru.

One night, good fortune came to Pizarro. A young prince of the royal Inca family walked into the Spanish camp. He was Manco Inca, a son of Huáscar. He was next in line for the throne. The young prince agreed to Pizarro's terms.

At Cuzco, the Spanish troops defeated any Incas who resisted. Pizarro moved into the city. It was November 15, 1533—a year to the day after Pizarro first gazed at the tents of Atahualpa, spread over the valley of Cajamarca.

The victorious Spanish officers moved into the Inca palaces. Francisco Pizarro even took over the one once used by the mighty Pachacuti.

Though Pizarro tried to slow their progress, the Spanish troops ran through the city, looting as they went. They filled warehouses with their treasure.

Manco Inca was crowned king. A 30-day festival followed. The hopeful Incas paraded their royal mummies in the streets. They sacrificed llamas as they had in the great days of their empire.

Believing Cuzco was firmly under Spanish control, Pizarro left for the Pacific coast. There he founded the seaport of Lima.

The Spaniards seemed in charge of all Peru. It looked as if the glorious days of the Inca civilization were over.

CHAPTER 9

An Empire in Hiding

■□□□□□□□□□□□

For a short time, Manco Inca ruled from the capital at Cuzco. But he was really under the control of Pizarro.

Soon this proud Inca grew tired of the ways of cruel conquerors. The Spanish had been ordering his every action for three years. They treated Manco Inca's people like slaves. Houses, gold, and even wives had been seized from them. They were forced to labor in mines and build monuments to the Spanish king. The living conditions for the once proud Incas were unacceptable.

Manco Inca secretly gathered Inca warriors from all over the nation. In May 1536, he

surprised the Spanish conquerors with a rebellion. His men attacked Cuzco and burned it. Withdrawing to the outskirts, they kept the 190 Spaniards in the city surrounded. Several times each week, either the Incas or the Spaniards would launch an attack. Men on both sides died. Almost a year went by.

Without training against horsemen with swords, the Incas began to lose ground. They withdrew into the mountains. Once hidden, Manco Inca continued to rule his people as best he could. Swiftly running down to the lowlands from their mountaintop, he and his men raided groups of Spaniards. And they killed any foreign travelers who came near their hiding places.

DANGEROUS STRANGERS

One day, seven weary Spanish soldiers trudged toward Manco Inca's mountain. Inca lookouts stopped them at a suspension bridge. They had deserted the Spanish army, the seven said. Would the Incas take them in?

Manco Inca helped them. He had a reason for this. He hoped they could teach his warriors to fight as the Spaniards did.

For many months, Manco Inca treated the seven men with dignity. Then, one day, while playing a game together called quoits, the seven Spaniards rushed Manco Inca. They pounded and stabbed him. As he died, Manco Inca named his young son, Sayri Tupac, to take his place.

Seeing their leader near death, nearby Inca warriors chased the Spaniards out of the city. A short distance away, they pulled the murderers from their horses and killed them.

Now it fell to the sons of Manco Inca to rule their people. One by one they attempted to do this.

Sayri Tupac, named leader by his father, was not a warlike young man. He enjoyed comforts and preferred peace. His father's friends and supporters helped him rule. But he had few ideas of his own. For ten years, there was little contact with the Spaniards.

In 1555, the Spanish viceroy at Cuzco sent gifts to Sayri Tupac. Would the young man come back to the capital and rule the Incas? Wealth and comfort were just what this young man wanted. So Sayri Tupac agreed to go to Cuzco.

He wore the red fringe of royalty, married a princess of royal blood, and became a Christian. But after two years in Cuzco, Sayri Tupac died. The Spanish viceroy claimed he was overwhelmed by a disease. But the Incas in their mountain retreat were sure he had been poisoned.

Another of Manco Inca's sons, Titu Cusi, was about 30 years old when Sayri Tupac died. Now he became Lord Inca. Remaining in the highlands, he kept his people safe from the Spaniards for 13 years. His holy men performed the old rites of the Sun. His bodyguards were jungle cannibals. He did allow Spanish priests to visit. But they could come only as far as the suspension bridges.

Typical Inca ruler

In 1569, a cruel new Spanish viceroy, Francisco de Toledo, came to Peru. He vowed he would finally finish off the Incas. Raising a large army, he stormed into the mountainous territory, guided by Inca defectors. His men burned thousands of idols, mummies, and quipus.

The huge Spanish army came closer and closer to the Inca retreat.

When Toledo's men reached the Inca highlands, they found that Titu Cusi had died a year before. His younger brother, Topa Amaru, was now Lord Inca.

To elude the Spaniards, Topa Amaru fled his hidden city. He escaped into the jungle. But the Spanish soldiers hunted him down. When Topa Amaru surrendered, he was holding the prized Inca image of the sun, Punchao. This was the sacred gold idol filled with the dust of the hearts of dead Lord Incas.

In the great square of Cuzco, Viceroy Toledo gave a signal. With a sweep of his arm, a swordsman beheaded Topa Amaru, the last Inca ruler.

Rulers of the Inca Empire After the Spanish Conquest 1533–1572

Topa Hualpa	son of Huayna Capac. He was briefly crowned by the Spaniards as a puppet king. The Spaniards probably poisoned him.
Manco Inca	son of Huayna Capac. He was crowned by Spaniards. In 1536, he rebelled and set up a government in the highlands. He was stabbed by Spanish deserters after 12 years as ruler.
Sayri Tupac	son of Manco Inca. Upon his father's death, he became Lord Inca. He ruled 1545–1558.
Titu Cusi	son of Manco Inca. He ruled the Inca jungle state and defied the Spaniards, 1558–1571.
Topa Amaru	son of Manco Inca. He was captured in the jungle and ordered executed by Spanish viceroy Toledo in 1572.

CHAPTER 10

A Lost City Is Found

After the Spanish viceroy Toledo ordered Topa Amaru beheaded, there was no longer a government in the highlands. Soon the jungle **reclaimed** the hidden settlements high in the Andes. Gradually, rooftops made of reeds rotted and blew away. Sun and wind eroded the edges of carefully cut stone buildings. Roots and trunks of towering trees sprouted and pushed their way through temples. A rain forest canopy enclosed whole villages.

The Incas had met with the Spanish conquerors from time to time during the 39 years after Atahualpa's death. But they had never invited the Spaniards into their hidden retreats. They always met their enemies at suspension bridges. For this reason, historians have found no evidence of Spanish influence in most hidden Andean towns. The Spanish simply never found them.

Atahualpa

In 1909, a history professor from the United States, Hiram Bingham, went to Peru in search of Inca ruins.

58

At first, he found very little of interest. But after he returned to his teaching, he often thought about Peru and its dramatic history.

Two years later in 1911, Professor Bingham returned to Peru. Hiring native guides, he spent months climbing steep cliffs and wading across dangerous rivers.

Exciting things began to happen as he moved farther from Cuzco. He found one ruin after another. Why, he wondered, was there no sign of Spanish visitors?

Bingham pressed on. He scaled more mountains. Sometimes, his journey stopped for days while workers chipped narrow trails along the mountainsides. Several times the trail gave way under his feet. Each day, he feared he might fall thousands of feet to the valley floor below.

At last, Hiram Bingham made a marvelous find. And it cost him only 50 cents!

After a six-day hike out of Cuzco, he camped near the hut of two Inca natives living far within the mountain peaks of the Andes. The Incas were growing crops on some terraces that appeared to be hundreds of years old.

Bingham asked his usual question. Were there Inca ruins nearby?

One of the natives told Bingham about some ruins at the

top of a steep cliff. He said they had been there for hundreds of years.

At first, the man did not want to guide the American to the ruins. He pointed straight up the mountain. He gestured that it was a hard, exhausting climb.

Bingham offered to pay the man, but the Inca still refused. Finally the offer reached 50 cents in Peruvian money. This was three times the ordinary daily wage for poor farmers. At last, the man agreed.

For hours, Bingham struggled to follow his guide up the steep mountain. Where there was no place for a trail, the Inca natives had placed notched logs to serve as primitive ladders. At the top, Bingham looked down. They had climbed 2,000 feet above the Indian's farm. And as Bingham turned away from the cliff, he had the surprise of his life!

He was standing on a row of terraces, each ten feet high. At his feet stretched the jungle in a bowl-shaped area. Certainly this had once been a city. It stretched between two jagged mountain peaks.

Machu Picchu

Machu Picchu

Bingham climbed down below the terraces. He pushed past rock work partly hidden by trees and moss. Here were walls built by master stoneworkers. He could sense the sacred feeling of the place.

In a book about his discovery, Bingham says, "We came to a great stairway. The sight held me spellbound. This was the principal temple. Would anyone believe what I had found?"

Professor Bingham had found the city of Machu Picchu. It was a huge sanctuary of the Inca empire. It was protected on three sides by steep slopes. It was also encircled by the fierce rapids of the Urubamba River far below.

This city had never been discovered by the Spaniards!

Historians believe the lost city served several purposes. Artifacts found there suggest it was the king's retreat. After the Spanish conquest, it became a refuge for the Chosen Women honored by the Incas. It was probably the ceremonial center for smaller villages hidden in the steep mountains.

Professor Bingham hired a large number of workers to help him study Machu Picchu. His workers tore out tough tangles of jungle growth and, in places, hardwood forest. Soon they had a better look at key buildings of the hidden

Temple of the Sun at Machu Picchu

city. They had discovered a royal palace, public buildings, and rows of houses. A Temple of the Sun closely resembled the one in Cuzco. Its stone walls were carefully crafted to curve in a semicircle.

More than 100 stairways connected the city's levels. Some had just three or four steps. But a few flights rose as many as 150 steps.

A major find was a huge *intihuatana*, or sundial, on the highest hill. In the Inca lands found earlier, all the intihuatanas had been broken and toppled over by the Spaniards. This one had not been touched.

Intihuatana at Machu Picchu

Hundreds of terraces, ten feet high, ringed the city. Here the Incas had grown their potatoes, corn, beans, quinoa, tomatoes, and sweet potatoes.

As usual, the Incas had taken great pains to use their water wisely. Several springs flowed from the mountains surrounding Machu Picchu. These were the principal water source for the city. A vast water system had been built here. Running along channels carved into rock, the diverted streams had provided moisture for the terraced crops. In the center of the city, baths and fountains filled themselves, using the same efficient water system.

Terraces at Machu Picchu

THE PALACE OF THE KING

Across the staircase from the curved Temple of the Sun was a group of buildings put together with special care. It is probable that no one but a king could have commanded such workmanship.

Of special note were the **lintels** over the doorways. They were made of solid granite and each weighed about three tons. Other doorways in the city also had granite lintels, but these were smaller in scale and could have been lifted into place by two or three men.

Lintel at Machu Picchu

Knowing that the Incas had no cranes, pulleys, or even beasts of burden, it is hard to imagine the placing of these three-ton palace lintels. It is likely the workmen built a solid inclined plane next to the wall. Perhaps they then raised the heavy lintels with levers, much the way the faraway Egyptians built the highest parts of their pyramids.

Bingham and his workers found great piles of broken pottery. Since so many of these pieces were located near the temple, it may be that they were broken as part of religious rituals. Many shawl pins were found in the houses.

Other dishes found in the city were made of circular stone pieces, carefully cut and polished. There were stone hammers and, in the oldest part of the city, five **obsidian** knives. Bingham found 100 specimens of Inca bronze, including axes, chisels, shawl pins, and knives.

There was no gold at Machu Picchu. Historians believe the city was stripped of its treasures during the struggle to produce Atahualpa's ransom to save his life.

PRESERVING THE DEAD OF MACHU PICCHU

Soon after Professor Bingham's workers finished clearing the city of its heavy jungle growth, he asked them to search for burial caves. The first one found was on a wooded slope on the eastern side of the ridge. The bones were those of a woman about 35 years old. She had been buried in the usual sitting position, with her knees drawn up under her chin. Her arms were folded around her shins. Buried with the mummy were her cooking pots and food containers.

Encouraged by this find, Bingham and the others searched other hillsides for burial caves. Their search was well rewarded.

The historians found more than 50 caves and 173 mummies. Of these mummies, 150 were women. This gave strength to the theory that Machu Picchu had been a haven for the Chosen Women after the conquest.

One body seemed to be that of a High Priestess, or *Mamacuna*. She was the person responsible for training the Chosen Women of Machu Picchu. Close to her bones were her personal belongings, her pottery, two shawl pins, and some sewing needles made from the spines of plants. At her side lay the skeleton of her dog, a breed much like a collie.

THE MYSTERY CONTINUES

Studying Machu Picchu has answered many questions about the last days of the Inca rulers. But still no one knows why and when the city was first occupied.

Many of the buildings must have been ordered built by Manco Inca and Titu Cusi in the 1550s to house the Chosen Women and their attendants. It is likely these were constructed in haste.

Inca ruler

64

But the finer temples and the palace are **elaborate**. They would have taken many decades to create.

People who have studied the Incas for many years believe the great king Pachacuti may have ordered the city built in the early 1400s. The center of his vast empire was in Cuzco. Machu Picchu, 50 miles away, would have provided protection against attackers that might have come from the river valley of the Urubamba.

Hiram Bingham wrote of his own theory concerning Machu Picchu. He was convinced that the older part of the city was established by Manco Capac, the first lord

Temple of the Sun at Machu Picchu

of Cuzco, as a site for a temple to his ancestors. He also believed that the semicircular Temple of the Sun in Cuzco, built in the 1400s, was a copy of the one in the ancient Inca city of Machu Picchu, not the other way around.

Whatever its beginnings, Machu Picchu was a vast, carefully guarded city where Incas defied the Spaniards by worshiping the sun, moon, thunder, and stars. It was there that the last four Lord Incas withdrew their followers to safety. And at Machu Picchu, the Chosen Women found a **refuge** from the Spanish conquerors.

Each year, thousands of visitors come to this best-preserved of all the Inca cities. Traveling by train, by bus, and on foot, they gaze in awe at this mystery in the Andes.

Historians continue to discover more about the history of the Incas. And yet, much of the mystery continues.

Glossary

artisan	craftsperson
cement	to bind together
conch	large sea mollusk
convent	building where a female religious order lives
descendant	person from a certain line of ancestors
elaborate	having a great deal of detail
embalmer	person who preserves a body
execute	to put to death
expand	to increase in size
fast	to not eat
ingot	mass of metal formed into a convenient shape for storage or transportation
irrigation	means of moving water from its source to a place that gets little moisture
lintel	horizontal beam over a door or window
loincloth	strip of cloth worn on the lower part of the body

loom	frame used for making cloth
mace	heavy spiked club
mortar	mixture that binds two bricks or stones together when it hardens
mummify	to preserve a body by drying
obsidian	hard black stone
poncho	blanketlike garment that has a slit and can be slipped over the head and worn as a sleeveless piece of clothing
province	division of a country; similar to a state
quarry	open area where stone is dug up
reclaim	to take back
refuge	safe place
staff	long stick carried in the hand; often used to aid walking
sundial	instrument that shows the time of day with a shadow
suspension bridge	bridge that is hung by cables and stretches from one tower to another
terrace	series of horizontal ridges in the side of a hillside. The top is leveled to provide additional space for farming.
trapezoid	four-sided figure with only two parallel sides
tribute	payment to show respect
tunic	simple slip-on garment that may or may not have sleeves
viceroy	governor of a country
wizardry	magical power

Index